Accessing Your Breakthrough

30 DAYS Of
PRAYER

Jack Carter Jr

Accessing Your Breakthrough

30 DAYS Of
PRAYER

Jack Carter Jr

McClure Publishing, Inc.

Jack Carter Copyright © 2024 at McClure Publishing, Inc.

All rights reserved. Printed and bound in the United States of America. According to the 1976 United States Copyright Act, no part of this book may be reproduced or utilized in any form or by any means, electronic or mechanical, including photocopying, recording, or by any information storage or retrieval system, except by a reviewer who may quote brief passages in a review to be printed in a magazine or newspaper, without permission in writing from the Publisher: Inquiries should be addressed to McClure Publishing, Inc. Permissions Department, 398 West Army Trail Road, Bloomingdale, IL 60108. First Printing: July 27, 2024.

Scriptures marked KJV are taken from the KING JAMES VERSION (KJV): KING JAMES VERSION, public domain.

Scriptures marked NIV are taken from the NEW INTERNATIONAL VERSION (NIV): Scripture taken from THE HOLY BIBLE, NEW INTERNATIONAL VERSION ●. Copyright© 1973, 1978, 1984, 2011 by Biblica, Inc.™. Used by permission of Zondervan.

Scriptures marked NLT are taken from the HOLY BIBLE, NEW LIVING TRANSLATION (NLT): Scriptures taken from the HOLY BIBLE, NEW LIVING TRANSLATION, Copyright© 1996, 2004, 2007 by Tyndale House Foundation. Used by permission of Tyndale House Publishers, Inc., Carol Stream, Illinois 60188. All rights reserved. Used by permission.

ISBN-13: 979-8-9907047-2-5

Book cover designed by TRIV Enterprise LLC

To order additional copies, please contact:

McClure Publishing, Inc.
https://McClurePublishing.com
800.659.4908

Dedication

This book is dedicated to my late father, Apostle Jack Carter Sr. 1949-2020, Who imparted a legacy of prayer to me. I am forever grateful. The mantle I carry was birthed out of a prayer room my Father would take me to regularly as a child. I would be the only child in the room, surrounded by praying adults. At the time, I had no idea what treasure I had received. I thought I was just a kid among some adults in a dusty, cloudy room. After years of development and growing in prayer, I now understand clearly that the prayer room was filled with the Glory of God.

Contents

Preface
Foreword
Introduction
Faith
Family
Finances
Freedom
Fire
Future
Protection
Fear
Relationship
Successful
Business
Health
Children
Ministry
World & Government
Important Decisions
Marriage
Deliverance
Mental Illness
Insecurities
Breaking Generational Curses
Releasing Generational Blessings
Overcoming Debt and Poverty
Breaking Strongholds
Peace
Strength
Overcoming Unforgiveness
Walking in Love
Shame
Anger and Rage

Preface

This book has been designed with you in mind. The focus of this book is not only to encourage and lift you out of any place you may be in, but the prayers in this book will also align you with the breakthrough God has planned for your life. It is time for you to access what God has for you. Far too long have you battled frustration from seasons and cycles of limitations.

This is your time. This is your opportunity to seize the breakthrough. Barriers are designed to constrain and restrict movement. God desires you to expand your borders and move beyond every limitation ever placed on you.

Micah 2:13 says, *The breaker is come up before them: they have broken up, and have passed through the gate, and are gone out by it: and their king shall pass before them, and the Lord on the head of them.* (KJV)

Whatever has held you back or caused you to lose time and momentum. I pray and prophesy that this book accelerates you into a life of breakthrough after breakthrough.

Foreword

Pastor Jack's 30-Day Prayer book
by Emmanuel Nnamani

This 30-day prayer book is very empowering and is recommended to anyone that wants to experience daily victories over issues and challenges of life through radical breakthrough prayers.

Using this book daily will help you to consistently engage in communion with God, and it will align you with a faith foundation that will enable you to prepare for daily victories and receive divine help from God through scripture inspired prayers that touches every area of human needs, including faith, family, finance, fruitfulness, forgiveness, protection, etc.

Emmanuel Nnamani, Lead Servant
Blessed for Life Ministries International
(International Missions and Watchman Prayer Network)

Introduction

If you are a believer, maintaining a healthy and victorious journey with the Lord is impossible without a steadfast commitment to prayer.

Prayer is the pulse and lifeline of the believer. When we make prayer a priority, it grants access to intimate encounters with God. Prayer eliminates distance from us and God. There are many valuable benefits of prayer. When we pray, it prevents us from becoming the enemy's prey. Prayer allows us to learn the heart and voice of God. Prayer also reveals the will of God. Prayer is not something God has designed for a select group of people. However, the Father's heart is that each of his children will establish a commitment to prayer.

God desires for each of us to commune with him. Communion with God is not an opportunity for God to hear us. More importantly, it's a reasonable time to listen to God. Luke 18:1 declares that men ought to always pray and not faint. Jesus can be seen throughout Scripture placing tremendous value on prayer. If prayer was Jesus's priority, it should inspire us to prioritize it.

In this book, you will discover anointed and powerful spirit-led prayers that will take you on a journey. I pray that as you pray these prayers by faith, you will experience life-changing breakthroughs.

I encourage you to approach these prayers with faith and enormous expectations for God to move and manifest in every area of your life.

There is something to be said about the nature of God. Many of us have experienced the rather calm side of God. God calms the sea. He speaks to the wind. He feeds 5,000 men who were hungry including women and children. The Lord opens the eyes of blind men, and he stopped the hemorrhaging of the woman with the issue of blood.

We heard of the baby in the manger. We even know of a rather loving and forgiving savior that while being mocked and hanging on a tree who took time to forgive a thief. Throughout scripture, we learn about the nature and character of our amazing God. He's gentle, kind, loving, merciful, forgiving, wise, and much more. However, there is another side of our Lord that doesn't get acknowledged and that is he's a breaker.

Jesus understood something that each of us must learn. Any legitimate breakthrough that will ever occur in our lives will only come through having FAITH in the breaker. Faith for a believer is the answer to accessing whatever we need and desire from God. Arm yourselves likewise because no matter who you are, your faith in God will be tested. Trusting God must be the priority of every believer. Why? Because the just shall live by faith. Your enemy doesn't want you trusting the Lord. Your faith in God is the key to gain access to every door the sovereign Lord has prepared for you.

Don't live your life under the assumption that God should be somewhere on your list of just in case. God should be the only one on your list. So many are living defeated lives because God or their faith in God is not prioritized.

You and I deserve to live a life of victory. A life that sets us apart from the bondage and oppression this world and the enemy of our destiny desperately wants us to live under.

Our breakthrough awaits us. The breaker wants you and I to live a life that allows us to live free mentally, emotionally physically, and spiritually. Have you had enough of the pressure and frustration of being so close but not reaching what belongs to you? So many things are fighting to keep you from walking through those doors. Your time is now to make intentional efforts and commitment to get your breakthrough. You have been wallowing in the struggle long enough. You've allowed yourself to be robbed far too long. The time to access your breakthrough is now. The most important thing to know is that God desires for you to live in the realm of breakthrough.

The realm of breakthrough is a place. I recall some time ago while driving a fully loaded late model vehicle. I attempted to pull off in the truck and each time I attempted to accelerate, the vehicle stopped abruptly preventing me from moving forward. For a moment, I was puzzled as to what was happening. Then I observed the door open *indication in the dashboard. The moment I completely closed the door. I was able to move forward.*

For so many of us in order for us to move forward or arrive to the place or realm of our breakthrough we need to close some doors we have open. It may be a door to an unhealthy relationship, a door to some unresolved issues, a door to some things we need to let go of that we know is unfruitful in our lives.

Once I closed the door that completely reset the safety feature in the vehicle, and I was able to move forward to my destination. It's time for you to allow the sovereign Lord the breaker to reset or set your life to the realm of breakthrough, so you can consistently live and experience the manifestation of breakthrough in your life.

There are things you and I will not encounter unless we access breakthrough. So how do you access breakthrough. Breakthrough ultimately is birthed through a desire or longing to go from one place to the next.

So often people will express how much they want breakthrough, but their words don't match their determination. Breakthrough is provoked by what you and I dominate and not what we tolerate. Sadly, we have all been guilty of tolerating seasons and cycles in our lives that have left us defeated and frustrated. Our days of feeling this way is over. This is our moment and our time for breakthrough. Our breakthrough is gonna come through connecting with the breaker in prayer. Prayer grants access to breakthrough because it's a portal to the power of God.

The power of God can breakthrough every barrier. Destroy every yoke and defeat every force that is working against you.

I Chronicles 14:11 So they came up to Baalperazim; and David smote them there. Then David said, God hath broken in upon mine enemies by mine hand like the breaking forth of waters: therefore, they called the name of that place Baalperazim. (KJV)

The place Baal-perazim in Hebrew means Lord of Breakthrough broken up of two words Baal meaning Lord perazim meaning breakthrough.

The previous verse 10 tells us that David enquired of the Lord. Prayer allows us to commune with God for guidance and direction. Once David enquired of the Lord, he received God's response that not only should he go forth against the Philistines, but God assured David he would be with him. Through David's prayer he received breakthrough.

Breakthrough will also come through pursing the presence of God.

There are so many times when the pressures of life is stacking against you and as a result you feel overwhelmed, a sudden loss of joy, burdened, and stuck. The presence of God is a realm that's attainable for all that remain in pursuit.

Psalm 16:11 *David declares that God will show him the path of life. That life David was referring to was life in the presence of God.*

This world can take a lot out of you but if you decide to embrace a life of continual joy, peace and victory, it can be found in the presence of God. That path is a worry free and carefree path that sets you apart to live the good life.

Access to our breakthrough can also come through our praise to God. Giving God praise marks us for breakthrough. Praise is speaking the language of God.

Psalm 22:3 says that God dwells in the praises of his people. God lives in our praises. You can't continually praise God and live apart from breakthrough. Praise is an invitation for God to breakthrough everything in your life that's trying to defeat you.

The Bible reveals something powerful about praise. The word of the Lord reveals in 2 Chronicles 20:22 That as the army of Jehoshaphat began singing praises unto the Lord, the Lord set an ambush for the army from Ammon, Moab and Mount Seir who had come to attack Judah. They were defeated.

In other words, there praise produced breakthrough and gave them victory over there enemy. God wants you to access your breakthrough more than you can ever imagine.

Let's go!

1

Trust God walk by faith, and you'll always be victorious.

FAITH

"But without faith, it's impossible to please him (God)."

Hebrews 11:6 (KJV)

Father, I thank you and praise you always. That the life I live in you through your son Jesus be a life of unwavering faith.

Your word says in Romans 1:17 that the just shall live by faith. So, Lord, today, I posture my heart and faith towards you, putting every situation before you. Lord, I believe you care for me, so I trust in your promise to be a very present help according to Psalm 46:1. Today, I intentionally resist fear and worry. Lord, I pray that you would render judgment against everything assigned to attack my faith. Father, I ask that you help me to continue letting go of all doubt and unbelief. Lord, help me to guard my heart, mouth, and ears from anything that is not of faith. As I live to please you, help me trust you completely in Jesus's Name.

> **I decree my faith and trust in the Lord is increasing daily.**

My Prayer Breakthrough Strategy

THE ENEMY....
_____
_____
_____
_____
_____
_____

MY BATTLEGROUND....
_____
_____
_____
_____
_____
_____

THE ENEMY'S STRATEGY....
_____
_____
_____
_____
_____
_____

MY PLAN OF ACTION....
_____
_____
_____
_____
_____
_____

God desires that your family be fruitful from generation to generation.

Family

"...But as for me and my household, we will serve the Lord."

Joshua 24:15 (NIV)

Father, I thank you for my family. God, I thank you for watching over my relatives and loved ones. Lord, I thank you for your hand in the lives of my family members. Lord, I honor you for the many blessings you have bestowed upon my family. Lord, I pray for the release of miracles and breakthroughs on behalf of my family. Father, I pray that every cycle and bloodline curse be broken off my family. Lord, I call on Jesus's mighty name to deliver my lost family members. I proclaim freedom and victory for my family. Lord, I pray against disunity and division in my family. Lord, I loose love and unity in my family. Lord, I put my family before you and intercede on their behalf. Father, let your wisdom rest in my family from this generation to the next and after that. Lord, I thank you that generational curses are broken, and bloodline blessings are flowing continually in the lives of my family. Father, I thank you that goodness and mercy are well acquainted with my family and follow each of them all the days of their lives. Lord, my family shall be called blessed because your blessings are on my family. Lord, I thank you that my family is free from premature death, sickness, and disease. Lord, I thank you that no weapon formed against my family shall prosper. Lord, I thank you for rendering every ungodly agenda and assignment against my family unsuccessful. Father, I thank you for your will, which shall be accomplished in the lives of my family in Jesus's Name.

> **I decree the blessings & protection of the Lord is upon my entire family.**

My Prayer Breakthrough Strategy

THE ENEMY....
_____
_____
_____
_____
_____
_____

MY BATTLEGROUND....
_____
_____
_____
_____
_____
_____

THE ENEMY'S STRATEGY....
_____
_____
_____
_____
_____
_____

MY PLAN OF ACTION....
_____
_____
_____
_____
_____
_____

There is no lack in God's Kingdom; God has an endless supply of provision for me.

Finances

"...Yea, Let them say continually, Let the Lord be magnified, which hath pleasure in the prosperity of his servant."
Psalm 35:27 (KJV)

Gracious and faithful Father, Lord, I thank you for your goodness and mercy, which shall follow me throughout my life as a grateful member of the family of God. Lord, I thank you for making me your responsibility. Lord, as I trust you and align myself with your promises, Lord, I thank you that you said you shall supply all of my needs. Lord, I thank you for your endless supply; I will never live in lack for the rest of my life. Lord, I pray that everything you bless me with, I will exercise good stewardship over it. Lord, I pray for wisdom to sow in the right direction so that I will harvest abundance and fruitfulness. Lord, I pray for the grace always to give cheerfully and never give to be seen. Lord, I pray for debt cancellation in my life. Lord, I pray that strongholds of generational poverty be broken off of my life. Lord, I thank you that the blessing is on my life, and it makes me rich and adds no sorrow. Lord, I pray for a cash anointing. That I will be able to pay cash for what I need and want. Lord, I thank you that my inheritance is the Lord. Through this inheritance, I'm the head and not the tail above only and not beneath the lender and not the borrower, and I pray that I will live in overflow for the rest of my life.

> **I declare and decree every cycle of lack is broken off of my life. I declare and decree I will live a life of abundance**

My Prayer Breakthrough Strategy

THE ENEMY....

_____
_____
_____
_____
_____
_____

MY BATTLEGROUND....

_____
_____
_____
_____
_____
_____

THE ENEMY'S STRATEGY....

_____
_____
_____
_____
_____
_____

MY PLAN OF ACTION....

_____
_____
_____
_____
_____
_____

4

> *God offers everyone liberty. Freedom is a choice, and you can choose to live free.*

Freedom

"If the Son Shall make you free, you shall be free indeed."
John 8:36 (KJV)

Father, I thank you for your Son Jesus; through his death, I received life, and his resurrection, I became free. Lord, I thank you for your plan for me to be free and live victorious in every area of my life. Lord, I pray that my mind will be transformed and renewed as I submit to your will. Lord, I pray for continual victory over temptations and strongholds. I pray that I will live free from all forms of lust, bitterness, unforgiveness, rage, rejection, slothfulness, pride, shame, ungodly affections, stealing, false burdens, men pleasing, self-pity, lying, fornication, adultery, manipulation, perversion, jealousy, and fear. I pray I will resist the enemy and fall out of agreement with every work of darkness. I pray that I will not fall victim to repetitive cycles of bondage and sin. Lord, I pray that I will not abuse the freedom that has been afforded to me by the blood of the lamb. Lord, I pray against generational and bloodline curses. Father, I thank you for divine health. Lord, I pray for freedom from all forms of sickness and disease. Lord, I pray against the sins and bondages of my father and grandfather, even unto the 3rd and 4th generations. Lord, I proclaim deliverance and freedom to be my portion, and I shall live victoriously in every area of my life.

I decree I will live a life of total freedom.

My Prayer Breakthrough Strategy

THE ENEMY.....
_____
_____
_____
_____
_____

MY BATTLEGROUND....
_____
_____
_____
_____
_____

THE ENEMY'S STRATEGY....
_____
_____
_____
_____
_____

MY PLAN OF ACTION....
_____
_____
_____
_____
_____

The Lord will purify your life to remove everything that aims to block you from living the beautiful life God desires for you to live.

Fire

"For our God is a consuming fire."
Hebrews 12:29 (KJV)

Gracious and faithful God. I thank you for being strong and mighty. I thank you for being undefeated. I thank you for being God alone. The Alpha and Omega, the Beginning and the End. Lord, I praise you for being God of the Angel armies. Lord, I thank you for being an all-consuming fire. I pray Lord that you release your fire into my life. Consume, Lord, everything that has been assigned to hinder me. Burn relentlessly everything that serves as a distraction and assignment to detour me from your glory. Lord, let your fire purify my heart. Lord, cause me to burn for you. Lord, I pray that you would ignite me to be a flame for you. Lord, as I remain lit, I pray that others will be affected by your fire in my life. Lord, let the release of your fire manifest in my walk with you, my purpose, home, family, finances, business, and ministry. I pray That my life will be governed by your fire. Lord, today and forever more, I pray to remain on fire for you.

I decree that my life will continually be refined and reflect the fire of God.

My Prayer Breakthrough Strategy

THE ENEMY....
_____
_____
_____
_____
_____

MY BATTLEGROUND....
_____
_____
_____
_____
_____

THE ENEMY'S STRATEGY....
_____
_____
_____
_____
_____

MY PLAN OF ACTION....
_____
_____
_____
_____
_____

God has a detailed plan for our lives, a plan that is good without any thoughts of hurting us. Embrace God's plan for your life by asking God to lead the way.

Future

"For I know the plans I have for you, declares the Lord, plans to prosper you and not to harm you, plans to give you hope and a future."
Jeremiah 29:11 (NIV)

Faithful God, I thank you for your plans for my life. Lord, I thank you for my life and times are in your hands. Gracious God, I thank you for pre-ordaining my life. Lord, I submit to your perfect will and plan for my future. Thank you, Father, for giving me great expectations for what you have prepared for me. I thank you, Lord, that eyes have not seen, nor have ears heard what you have in store for me. Lord, I thank you that no agenda of hell will sabotage or veto the plans you have for me. Lord, I thank you for covering my destiny and my future in the blood of Jesus.

Lord, my future is filled with increase, fruitfulness, abundance, and success. Lord, I thank you that what's to come is far greater than what has been. Lord, I thank you that my life is in your hands and the evil one can't pluck me out. Lord, I thank you that you will be with me always even into my future. Lord, I thank you for setting goodness and mercy in place to follow me into my future and all the days of my life.

> **I declare over my life that the perfect plan and will of God are manifesting daily.**

My Prayer Breakthrough Strategy

THE ENEMY....
_____
_____
_____
_____
_____

MY BATTLEGROUND....
_____
_____
_____
_____
_____

THE ENEMY'S STRATEGY....
_____
_____
_____
_____
_____

MY PLAN OF ACTION....
_____
_____
_____
_____
_____

7

Nothing can penetrate the divine protection of God.

Protection

"No weapon that is formed against [me] shall prosper...."
Isaiah 54:17 (KJV)

Heavenly Father, I thank you for your unconditional love toward me. I call you Abba because you are my Father. Lord, I thank you for being my protector as a Father. A protector that shields and guards me from my enemies. Lord, I thank you that your protection causes my enemies to stumble and fall. Lord, I thank you for your protection, which causes weapons that are formed against me not to prosper. Lord, I thank you for being my defense; my enemies are your enemies. Lord, I thank you for even assigning angels to have charge over me. Lord, I thank you that I am surrounded and protected by your love. Lord, I thank you. As a good Father, you have made me your responsibility. Lord, I thank you for protecting me from seen and unseen danger. Lord, I thank you that I do not have to fear because you are with me. Lord, I trust you at your word and believe every promise you gave me to protect me. I thank you for your divine protection and your eyes watching over me in Jesus's Name.

I declare God is my protection, and everywhere I go, I believe God has covered me.

My Prayer Breakthrough Strategy

THE ENEMY....
_____
_____
_____
_____
_____
_____

MY BATTLEGROUND....
_____
_____
_____
_____
_____
_____

THE ENEMY'S STRATEGY....
_____
_____
_____
_____
_____
_____

MY PLAN OF ACTION....
_____
_____
_____
_____
_____

Fear has a voice that aims to talk you into being afraid. Silence fear by refusing to come into agreement with it and live a life of victory.

Fear

"For God hath not given us the spirit of fear; but of power, and of love, and of a sound mind."
2 Timothy 1:7 (KJV)

Faithful and merciful God, I honor you and your gracious love for me. I thank you for giving me a sound mind. Lord, I thank you for proclaiming victory over every situation in my life today. Lord today I ask that you forgive me for any worry or fear that I have allowed to enter my life. Today, Lord, I fall out of agreement with fear and embrace your love for me. Lord, I receive your peace in exchange for fear. Lord, I thank you for renewing my mind and removing all mental conflict from my thought life. Lord, I thank you for giving me power over fear and freeing me from all cycles of worry. Lord, I thank you for healing my mind and delivering me from fright, phobias, and terror. Lord, I thank you for restoring my faith and allowing me to believe in your everlasting love. Today, I proclaim victory over fear. Lord, I thank you for giving me the courage not to be afraid to live the life you have planned for me. In Jesus Name.

> **I declare that I am free from fear, and I will not be afraid. God is with me, and I will live victoriously all the days of my life.**

My Prayer Breakthrough Strategy

THE ENEMY....
_____
_____
_____
_____
_____
_____

MY BATTLEGROUND....
_____
_____
_____
_____
_____
_____

THE ENEMY'S STRATEGY....
_____
_____
_____
_____
_____
_____

MY PLAN OF ACTION....
_____
_____
_____
_____
_____
_____

God is in the business of framing our lives with healthy and productive relationships.

Relationship

"Therefore encourage one another and build each other up, just as you are doing."
I Thessalonians 5:11 (NIV)

Lord, I thank you for always being faithful. Father, thank you for being concerned about every detail of my life, even my relationships. Lord, I thank you for divine connections and partnerships. Lord, I thank you for establishing healthy relationships. Lord, I thank you for ordaining relationships that hold me accountable, encourage me, and build me up. Thank you for relationships that help bring out the best in me and not the worst in me. Lord, I thank you for blessing my relationships. Father, I thank you for causing me to be careful for nothing. Lord, I thank you for blessing me to walk with those who seek wisdom. Lord, I thank you for a circle of support. Lord, I thank you for protecting me from relationships that don't reflect your purpose and plan for my life. Lord, I thank you for removing those from my life who seek my demise. Lord, I thank you for connecting me with people that want to see me blessed. I thank you God for giving me discernment and the wisdom to recognize unhealthy and unfruitful relationships in advance. Lord you have been kind, always loving and never falling short of your word. I praise you always for guarding me, covering me and protecting me from the wrong relationships. I'm grateful for your concern and care for me.

I decree I will enjoy a life of outstanding relationships.

My Prayer Breakthrough Strategy

THE ENEMY....
_____
_____
_____
_____
_____
_____

MY BATTLEGROUND....
_____
_____
_____
_____
_____
_____

THE ENEMY'S STRATEGY....
_____
_____
_____
_____
_____
_____

MY PLAN OF ACTION....
_____
_____
_____
_____
_____

10

*God has built you for success.
It's a part of your DNA.*

Successful

"Study this Book of Instruction continually. Meditate on it day and night so you will be sure to obey everything written in it. Only then will you prosper and succeed in all you do."
Joshua 1:8 (NLT)

Father, I thank you for your plan for my life. I thank you, Lord, that your will is that I would prosper and have great success. Lord, I receive your will, and I agree with your plan for my life. Lord, I surrender to every process that produces your promise over my life. Lord, I pray that your word will never depart from me, for in it, I shall have great success. Lord, I pray that I will seek you always. As I seek you Lord I thank you that I will always prosper. Lord, I pray for wisdom to uphold the success you grant me. Lord, I pray that you help me remain humble no matter the height or width of my success. Lord help me always to consider those who have helped me on my journey. Lord, I pray that I will have a heart to help those in need. Lord use me to be a blessing. Father, I pray for success to let my light shine before men that you would be praised. Lord let me establish success that will become a legacy. Lord help me see success through your eyes and not through the eyes of man. Lord grant me success in every area of my life for your glory. In Jesus name amen.

I decree and declare God has given me a blueprint for success.

My Prayer Breakthrough Strategy

THE ENEMY....
_____
_____
_____
_____
_____
_____

MY BATTLEGROUND....
_____
_____
_____
_____
_____
_____

THE ENEMY'S STRATEGY....
_____
_____
_____
_____
_____
_____

MY PLAN OF ACTION....
_____
_____
_____
_____
_____

11

God makes the perfect business partner. Invite Holy Spirit to lead you in every business decision.

Business

"Commit your actions to the Lord, and your plans will succeed."
Proverbs 16:3 (NLT)

Gracious Lord, I thank you for your love and grace toward me. Lord, I thank you for giving me favor with both you and man. Lord, I thank you for your plan for my life as an entrepreneur, which is wrapped in prayer and faith. As I trust and acknowledge you in every business decision, I thank you for ordering my steps. I thank you for giving me the courage not to be afraid to step out on your word. I pray that I will be faithful over the small beginnings and honor you with every increase. I pray that I will always exercise wisdom, be integral, and remain teachable. Lord, I pray for a business that reflects you in every way. I pray that the service I provide will tremendously bless the lives of others. I pray that you would render and execute judgment against any attack or plan to sabotage my business. Lord, I pray that Holy Spirit would be my business partner and Chief Executive Officer (CEO) to lead me and guide me in all my business decisions. Father help me to always provide quality service with integrity. God let everything I do be unto you. Lord grant me grace in meetings and boardrooms to close significant deals. God expose me to first class so that I will render first class to others. I proclaim great success in business as I choose to always keep you first.

I decree and declare God has positioned me to have great success in my business.

My Prayer Breakthrough Strategy

THE ENEMY....
_____
_____
_____
_____
_____
_____

MY BATTLEGROUND....
_____
_____
_____
_____
_____
_____

THE ENEMY'S STRATEGY....
_____
_____
_____
_____
_____
_____

MY PLAN OF ACTION....
_____
_____
_____
_____

God desires you to live healthy and whole. What you were purposed to do requires both your spiritual and physical vitality.

Health

"Beloved, I [would] above all things that thou mayest prosper and be in health, even as thy soul prospereth."

III John 1:2 (KJV)

Heavenly Father, today and always, I honor you. I glorify you for who you are and all that you have done. I thank you for creating me for your glory. I yield every part of me to you. My mind is yours; my body is yours, my spirit is yours. You have paid the ultimate price for my life. Your purchase is greatly appreciated, and I honor you with my life. I thank you for your good health. I pray that my entire anatomy will function as you designed it. I pray that no sickness or disease will touch or contaminate this body. I pray that you help me to be a good steward over my body. I pray that I will eat right, exercise, laugh often and not allow stress to rule in my life. I pray that my mind will be free of mental conflict and distress. I pray that I will keep my mind stayed on you so that I will be kept in perfect peace. I pray that every generational and bloodline curse of sickness and disease is broken off of my life and the life of my children and every generation thereafter. Lord, I thank you that my desire aligns with your desire for me to be in good health. I thank you Lord that because of Jesus's stripes every diagnoses and negative report regarding my health will be overturned. I will remain in good health and live in your promises all the days of my life.

> **I decree and declare I will live with discipline while leading a strong and healthy life.**

My Prayer Breakthrough Strategy

THE ENEMY....

_____
_____
_____
_____
_____

MY BATTLEGROUND....

_____
_____
_____
_____
_____

THE ENEMY'S STRATEGY....

_____
_____
_____
_____
_____

MY PLAN OF ACTION....

_____
_____
_____
_____
_____

13

God knows your love for your children. God has an even more profound love for your children and desires to see them live a blessed life.

Children

"Children obey your parents in the Lord, for this is right. 'Honor your father and mother'—which is the first commandment with a promise—"
Ephesians 6:1-2 (NIV)

Father, I thank you for your Grace and your goodness. I thank you for the life of my children. Lord, I thank you for watching over them. Lord, I pray for your divine protection over my son/daughter. Lord God, I pray my children will flourish in creativity and education. Lord, I pray that my children will have great success. Lord, I pray that my son/daughter will know their identity and purpose. Lord, cause my children to abound in prosperity. Lord, I pray for the wisdom to parent my children and the ability to help them cultivate their gifts and talents. Lord, give me the grace to cover and care for my children. Lord, your word declares excellent shall be the peace of our children. God, I pray that the peace of God will rest on my children. Lord, bless the thought life of my children. Lord, I pray my children will hunger for you and delight in your way. Lord, I pray for God's favor in my children's lives. Lord, let your goodness and mercy follow my children throughout their lives. Lord, I pray that generational curses be broken off of my children and generational blessings be released. Father, I pray that my child will never bring shame on my name. Lord, I pray that you preserve the lives of my children. Father I bind premature death and Lord, I pray that no sickness or disease will claim their lives. Lord, I pray for the company they keep. Lord surround my sons and daughters with positive influence. Father, I pray that my children will have no desire for the company of evildoers. Lord, I pray that my children will remain in your hand so that the enemy can't pluck them out. Lord, I pray that my children will always honor me and rise up and call me blessed. Lord, I pray that my children will always reverence you. Lord, I pray that your glory will be manifested in the lives of my children. In Jesus's name.

> **I declare and decree my son/daughter will honor God with their lives.**

My Prayer Breakthrough Strategy

THE ENEMY....
_____
_____
_____
_____
_____
_____

MY BATTLEGROUND....
_____
_____
_____
_____
_____
_____
_____

THE ENEMY'S STRATEGY....
_____
_____
_____
_____
_____
_____
_____

MY PLAN OF ACTION....
_____
_____
_____
_____
_____
_____

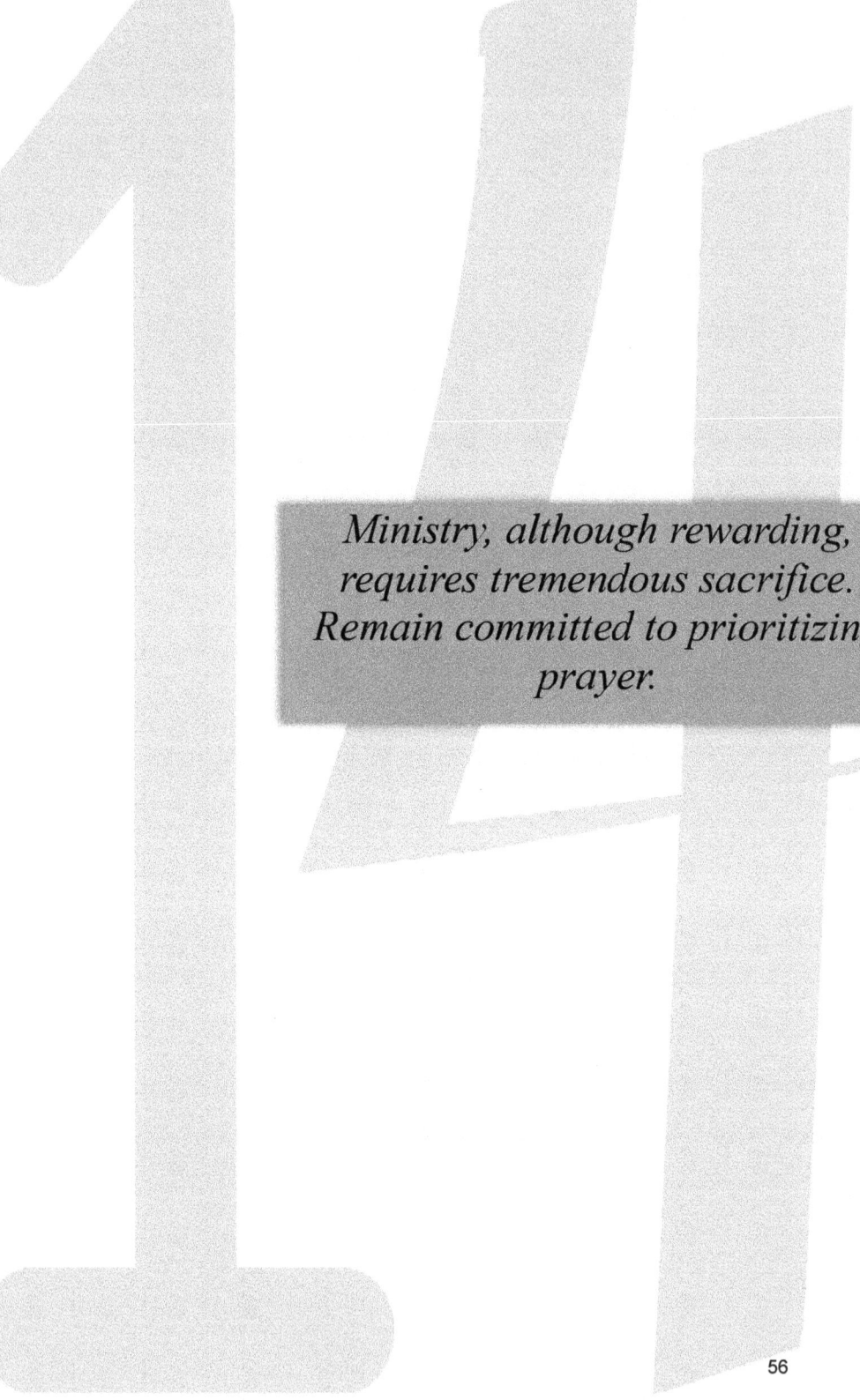

Ministry, although rewarding, requires tremendous sacrifice. Remain committed to prioritizing prayer.

Ministry

"Therefore seeing we have this ministry, as we have received mercy, we faint not;"
II Corinthians 4:1 (KJV)

Father, I thank you for your goodness and faithfulness towards me. Lord, I thank you for making me and calling me to do work for you while I was in my mother's womb. Lord, I agree with your word that I shall do more significant works and continue the work of Jesus on the earth. I pray that the ministry you have chosen me for will impact lives, communities, cities, states, and nations. Father, in the name of Jesus, I submit to every process that will help develop and mature me in ministry. Father, I pray that I will never seek to please man but only you Lord. Lord, I pray that I will never succumb to pride or complacency in ministry. Lord, I pray that I will always prioritize love for you and your people. Lord, I pray that I will not succumb to weariness in well-doing. Lord, I thank you that I have great success in ministry as I walk in your anointing, stand on truth and seek to continually do your will.

> **I decree and declare that the hand of God is on my life, my purpose, and my ministry.**

My Prayer Breakthrough Strategy

THE ENEMY....
_____
_____
_____
_____
_____

MY BATTLEGROUND....
_____
_____
_____
_____
_____

THE ENEMY'S STRATEGY....
_____
_____
_____
_____
_____

MY PLAN OF ACTION....
_____
_____
_____
_____
_____

Every problem in our world can always be traced back to a lack of prayer. Continue to pray for our world.

World & Government

"If my people, who are called by my name, will humble themselves and pray and seek my face and turn from their wicked ways, then I will hear from heaven, and I will forgive their sin and will heal their land."

II Chronicles 7:14

Lord, I thank you for your goodness and your mercy toward us. Father, I intercede on behalf of our world and the government of the nations of this world. Lord, I thank you that your eyes are in every place beholding the good and the evil. Lord, I pray that you would judge every wicked thing that has been assigned to insight and promote evil in the world and the governments of the nations of our world. Lord, your word declares that the heart of the king is in your hand. So, Lord, I pray that you would turn the hearts of world leaders toward you. Lord, I pray that believers across the world would be burdened with a passion to pray for our world. I pray against the hearts and motives of evildoers in positions of power that thrive off evil working. Lord, I pray for an increase of righteous men/woman in positions of power. Lord, your word says, "When the just are in position the people rejoice." Lord, I pray against laws that have been instituted to negatively impact the people. Lord, you said, "If we pray you would heal our land." So, I pray that the prayers and cries of your people be heard. So that the people of the earth will know of your goodness, mercy, and love toward us in Jesus's name.

I declare and decree the will of God is advancing in our world.

My Prayer Breakthrough Strategy

THE ENEMY....

_____
_____
_____
_____
_____
_____

MY BATTLEGROUND....

_____
_____
_____
_____
_____
_____

THE ENEMY'S STRATEGY....

_____
_____
_____
_____
_____

MY PLAN OF ACTION....

_____
_____
_____
_____
_____

God is concerned about every detail of your life and desires us to make quality decisions that will positively impact our path.

Important Decisions

"In all thy ways acknowledge him, and he shall direct thy paths."
Proverbs 3:6 (KJV)

Father, in the name of Jesus, I thank you and honor you for your faithfulness towards me. You said you will never forsake me, so I call your great name. Lord, you said you will be a present help for me in time of need. Lord, I need you to help me make the right decisions. Lord, you said the Lord orders the steps of a good man/woman. So, help me to move in the right direction. Lord, I pray that my motives will remain pure, and my heart aligns with truth as I make this critical decision. Lord, I pray for wisdom and understanding as I choose to make the right choice. Lord, increase my discernment and let me not be in conflict with things that are not in my best interest. I thank you, Lord, for ordering my steps and causing your word to be a light unto my feet and a lamp unto my path in Jesus's name.

I decree and declare the wisdom of God governs my life to make quality decisions.

My Prayer Breakthrough Strategy

THE ENEMY....
_____
_____
_____
_____
_____
_____

MY BATTLEGROUND....
_____
_____
_____
_____
_____
_____

THE ENEMY'S STRATEGY....
_____
_____
_____
_____
_____
_____

MY PLAN OF ACTION....
_____
_____
_____
_____
_____

17

Marriage is a gift, cherish it, and God will preserve it.

Marriage

> "So they are no longer two, but one flesh. Therefore, what God has joined together, let no one separate."
> Matthew 19:6 (NIV)

Lord, I thank you for my marriage. Lord, thank you for allowing my spouse and me to become one. Lord, I pray that you continually bless and favor my spouse and I on our marriage journey. Lord, help me always to honor, respect, and value my mate. Lord, I pray that I will always listen and support my spouse. Lord, I pray that you will give my spouse and I wisdom to quickly resolve any dispute or conflict in our marriage. Lord, teach me how to love my spouse more and more. Lord, I pray that our home will be filled with peace, love, and unity. Lord, I decree the enemy cannot have my marriage. Lord, I pray that my spouse and I will be an example to others of what true love looks like. Lord, I pray that my spouse and I will remain faithful, and committed to one another. Lord, keep your hand on our marriage that we will continue to walk and live in unconditional love towards each other.

> **I decree and declare my marriage is blessed, fruitful, and full of bliss.**

My Prayer Breakthrough Strategy

THE ENEMY....
_____
_____
_____
_____
_____
_____

MY BATTLEGROUND....
_____
_____
_____
_____
_____
_____

THE ENEMY'S STRATEGY....
_____
_____
_____
_____
_____
_____

MY PLAN OF ACTION....
_____
_____
_____
_____
_____

God is a strong deliverer. Nothing you will ever face in your life will surpass God's ability to bring you out.

Deliverance

"And it shall come to pass, that whosoever shall call on the name of the Lord shall be delivered: for in [M]ount Zion and in Jerusalem shall be deliverance, as the Lord said, and in the remnant whom the Lord shall call."
Joel 2:32 (KJV)

Lord, I thank you for being my deliverer, for I know deliverance comes from the Lord. So, I submit myself entirely to your spirit. Holy Spirit, rule, rest, and abide in me. Lord, I ask you to reside in me. Destroy every yoke, bondage, and burden in my life. In the name of Jesus, free me from all past and present bondage. Father, I love you and believe you desire for me to live free from everything that's not like you. Lord, deliver me from every stronghold, weight, and sin that so easily beset me. Lord, help me to live victoriously and not entangle myself again with any yoke of bondage. In the mighty name of Jesus.

> **I decree and declare I will live free in every area of my life.**

My Prayer Breakthrough Strategy

THE ENEMY....
_____
_____
_____
_____
_____
_____

MY BATTLEGROUND....
_____
_____
_____
_____
_____
_____

THE ENEMY'S STRATEGY....
_____
_____
_____
_____
_____

MY PLAN OF ACTION....
_____
_____
_____
_____
_____

10

Whatever you focus on grows. The soil of your mind deserves good seeds. Plant healthy thoughts.

Mental Illness

"Thou wilt keep him in perfect peace, whose mind is stayed on thee: because he trusts in thee."
Isaiah 26:3 (KJV)

Father, I thank you for your goodness and love toward me. Lord, I thank you for your plan for my life: to live in perfect peace. Lord, I thank you that you help me keep my mind on you daily. I am free from all mental conflict. Lord, I thank you that my mind is clear and free from worry, anxiety, fear, confusion, stress, strife, doubt, shame, self-pity, insecurity, self-harm, jealousy, bitterness, envy, and anger. Thank you for loving me enough to give me peace, joy, and gladness. I pray that my life will remain full of the joy of the Lord. I decree that I will not succumb to condemnation to sadness, depression, discouragement, offense, or hurts. I love you, Lord, and I thank you that my heart and mind is healthy and whole.

> **I decree and declare my mind is filled with peace and free from mental conflict.**

My Prayer Breakthrough Strategy

THE ENEMY....
_____
_____
_____
_____
_____
_____

MY BATTLEGROUND....
_____
_____
_____
_____
_____
_____

THE ENEMY'S STRATEGY....
_____
_____
_____
_____
_____
_____

MY PLAN OF ACTION....
_____
_____
_____
_____
_____
_____

Being made in the image of God allows us the privilege to glory in the wonderful work God has established in our lives.

Insecurities

"I praise you because I am fearfully and wonderfully made; your works are wonderful, I know that full well."
Psalm 139:14 (NIV)

Father, I thank you that I am fearfully and wonderfully made. Lord, I thank you for your love for me, which endures forever. Lord, I pray that I will remain a constant reminder of your love. Lord, I pray that I will not allow negative words from my past or present to reflect how I view myself. Lord, I pray that you remove insecurity and intimidation from me. Lord, I pray that I will be confident in who you created me to be and the plan you have for my life. Lord, I pray I will not compare myself to anyone but always find joy in your hand on my life. Lord, I pray that I will be free from all insecurities and self-doubt. Lord, I pray for confidence and boldness to live out my God-given purpose.

> **I decree and declare that I will not live in insecurity, but remember I am fearfully and wonderfully made.**

My Prayer Breakthrough Strategy

THE ENEMY....
_____
_____
_____
_____
_____
_____

MY BATTLEGROUND....
_____
_____
_____
_____
_____
_____

THE ENEMY'S STRATEGY....
_____
_____
_____
_____
_____
_____

MY PLAN OF ACTION....
_____
_____
_____
_____
_____
_____

21

The mercy and blessings of God do not end with one generation.

Breaking Generational Curses

"Christ redeemed us from the curse of the law by becoming a curse for us, for it is written: 'Cursed is everyone who is hung on a pole.'"
Galatians 3:13 (NIV)

Father, in the name of Jesus, I thank you for having proven yourself faithful in many ways. You are my provider, promise keeper, and protector. Lord, I thank you as my savior and sovereign Lord for giving me power over all the works of the devil. So, Lord, I pray against every bloodline curse against my family line. I pray that every sin be forgiven, and every bloodline curse be broken. Lord, I pray deliverance and healing to flow unrestricted through my bloodline. Father in the name of Jesus I bind up every assignment of Hell against my bloodline and I loose the purposes and plan of God for my family. Lord, I pray against every ungodly cycle and pattern that has been released against my family and generation to come. Father I pray that restraints and hindrances that has held my family back for generations be broken. God I thank you for causing breakthrough to be my portion. Lord, I thank you that who the son has made free is free indeed. Through that freedom I decree generational blessings over my family and bloodline. I decree divine health and prosperity over my bloodline in Jesus name.

> **I decree and declare every generational curse is broken off of my family, and generational blessings are flowing from generation to generation.**

My Prayer Breakthrough Strategy

THE ENEMY....
_____
_____
_____
_____
_____
_____

MY BATTLEGROUND....
_____
_____
_____
_____
_____
_____

THE ENEMY'S STRATEGY....
_____
_____
_____
_____
_____
_____

MY PLAN OF ACTION....
_____
_____
_____
_____
_____

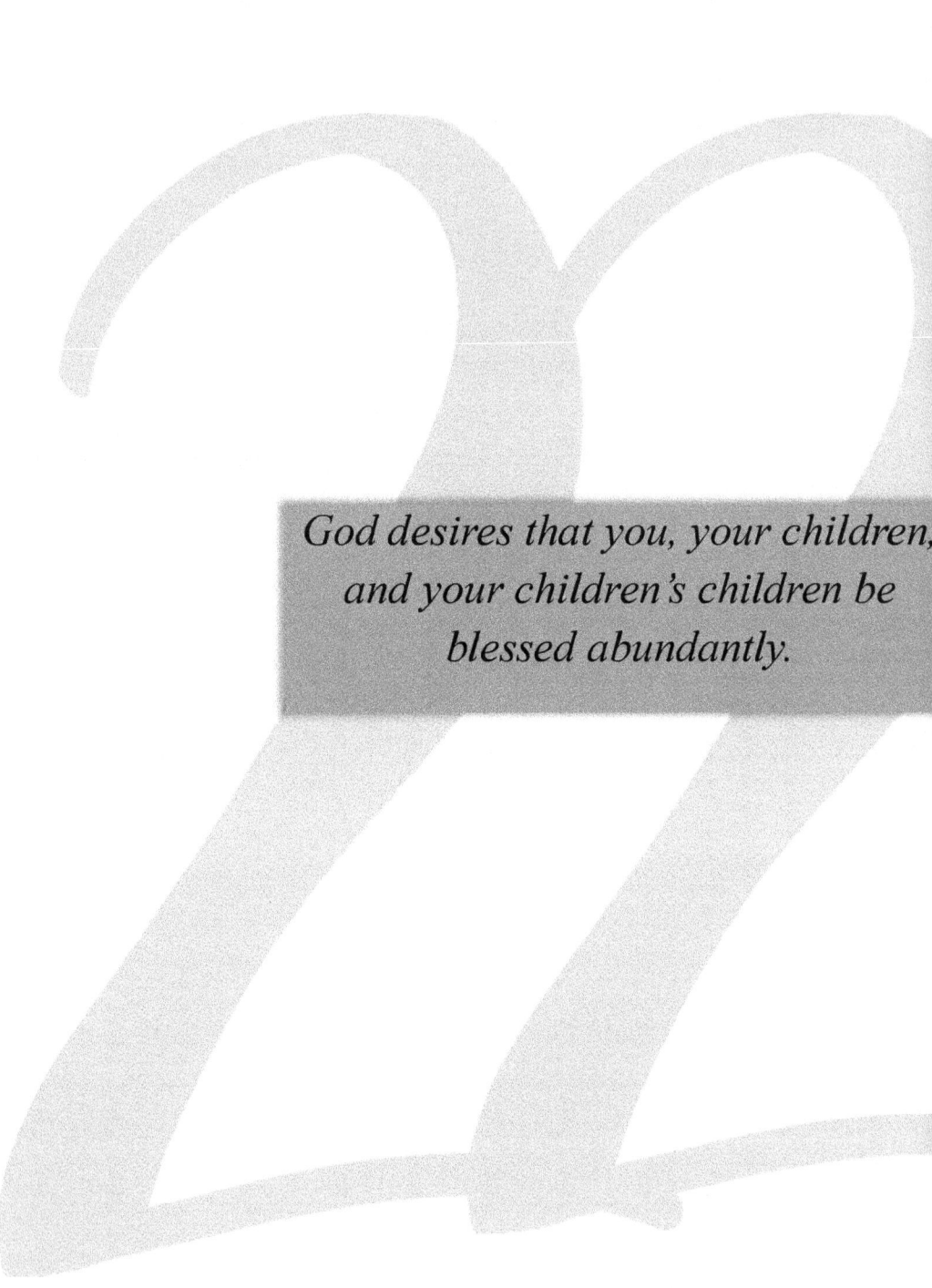

God desires that you, your children, and your children's children be blessed abundantly.

Releasing Generational Blessings

"...Blessed are those who fear the Lord, who find great delight in his commands, their children will be mighty in the land; the generation of the upright will be blessed."
Psalm 112:1-2 (NIV)

Father, in the name of Jesus, I proclaim that life and death are in the power of my tongue. I thank you, Lord, that it shall be established if I decree a thing. Lord, I decree generational blessings over my household, family, and bloodline. Lord, I pray and release the bloodline blessing of salvation. Lord, I decree an intimate and sincere relationship with you for my son and daughter, their children and their children's children. Lord, I decree the anointing and grace of prophetic mantles, glory carriers, true worshippers, preachers, teachers, evangelists, and intercessors to come through my bloodline. Lord, I pray for successful, integral business, men and women, to flow through my bloodline. I pray and release blessings to conquer the Seven Mountains of Influence: Mountain of Business, Arts/Entertainment, Media, Government, Family, Education, and Religion. Lord, I pray that my bloodline will flourish and thrive, and the blessing of the Lord will manifest richly and abundantly in my family.

> **I decree and declare that the blessings of God rest on my family from generation to generation.**

My Prayer Breakthrough Strategy

THE ENEMY....
_____
_____
_____
_____
_____
_____

MY BATTLEGROUND....
_____
_____
_____
_____
_____
_____

THE ENEMY'S STRATEGY....
_____
_____
_____
_____
_____
_____

MY PLAN OF ACTION....
_____
_____
_____
_____
_____

23

God has empowered you to prosper. Choose to position yourself for a life of prosperity.

Overcoming Debt and Poverty

"Good planning and hard work lead to prosperity, but hasty shortcuts lead to poverty."
Proverbs 21:5 (NLT)

Father, in the name of Jesus, I thank you, Lord. Thank you for becoming poor so that I may be rich. Lord, I thank you for your word, which declared I am to owe no man anything but love. So, Lord, I pray that debt and poverty will not govern my life. Lord, I pray for grace to manage what you bless me with. Lord, I pray I will not live from check to check but will always have more than enough. Lord, I pray for the grace to be a giver and a sower by the leading of the Lord. Lord, I pray that I will be wise in all my business and financial endeavors. Lord, I pray that lack will never be my portion, and I will always live in increase, overflow, and abundance. Lord, I pray by your power I am free from all poverty mindsets and thought patterns. Lord, let your blessings overtake me, Lord and cause all setbacks and cycles of poverty to be broken off my life. Lord, I pray your will for me to prosper to manifest exceedingly abundantly and above all I can ever ask or think.

> **I decree and declare I am an overcomer. I decree debt, and poverty is not my portion. I will live in prosperity all the days of my life.**

My Prayer Breakthrough Strategy

THE ENEMY....
_____
_____
_____
_____
_____
_____

MY BATTLEGROUND....
_____
_____
_____
_____
_____
_____

THE ENEMY'S STRATEGY....
_____
_____
_____
_____
_____
_____

MY PLAN OF ACTION....
_____
_____
_____
_____
_____

Freedom is a priority of God for each of our lives. Don't hold on to or allow anything to hold on to you that will lock you out of your purpose and promises.

Breaking Strongholds

"(For the weapons of our warfare are not carnal, but mighty through God to the pulling down of strong holds;)"

II Corinthians 10:4 (KJV)

Father God, in the name of Jesus, I thank you that you have come to set the captives free. Lord, I thank you that your word reveals who the son sets free is free indeed. Lord, thank you for letting me know that liberty is my portion. I pray that every stronghold in my life is broken. Lord, your word declares that the anointing destroys yokes. I decree and declare that every yoke, bondage, and stronghold is broken off of my life. Lord, I disagree with every lie, word curse, and chatter negativity spoken over my life. Lord, I pray for grace to identify and be free from strongholds of death, destruction, and delay. I pray against every stronghold that has come to sabotage my ability to hear and see you clearly. I pray for liberation and total freedom over every stronghold. I pray, Lord, that your word will be established in my heart, leading me to a life of sweatless victory.

> **I decree and declare that I am free from bondage and all strongholds that seek to bind me.**

My Prayer Breakthrough Strategy

THE ENEMY....
_____
_____
_____
_____
_____
_____

MY BATTLEGROUND....
_____
_____
_____
_____
_____
_____

THE ENEMY'S STRATEGY....
_____
_____
_____
_____
_____
_____

MY PLAN OF ACTION....
_____
_____
_____
_____

25

> *Make peace a priority, and don't allow anything to rob you of it.*

Peace

"And he arose, and rebuked the wind, and said unto the sea, Peace, be still. And the wind ceased, and there was a great calm."
Mark 4:39 (KJV)

Father God, in the name of Jesus, I thank you for filling my life with peace. Peace in my mind, peace in my heart, peace in my will, peace in my conversation, peace surrounds me, and peace is my priority. Lord, I pray that you will help me govern my life peacefully. Lord, I pray that as your spirit leads me, peace will continually be my portion. Lord, help me to guard my peace from negative people and toxic environments. Lord, help me to understand how frail I am so that my life will be a fountain of peace flowing from me day to day. Lord, I praise and worship you for your unfailing love that helps me to remain in perfect peace.

> **I decree and declare peace is my portion.**

My Prayer Breakthrough Strategy

THE ENEMY....

MY BATTLEGROUND....

THE ENEMY'S STRATEGY....

MY PLAN OF ACTION....

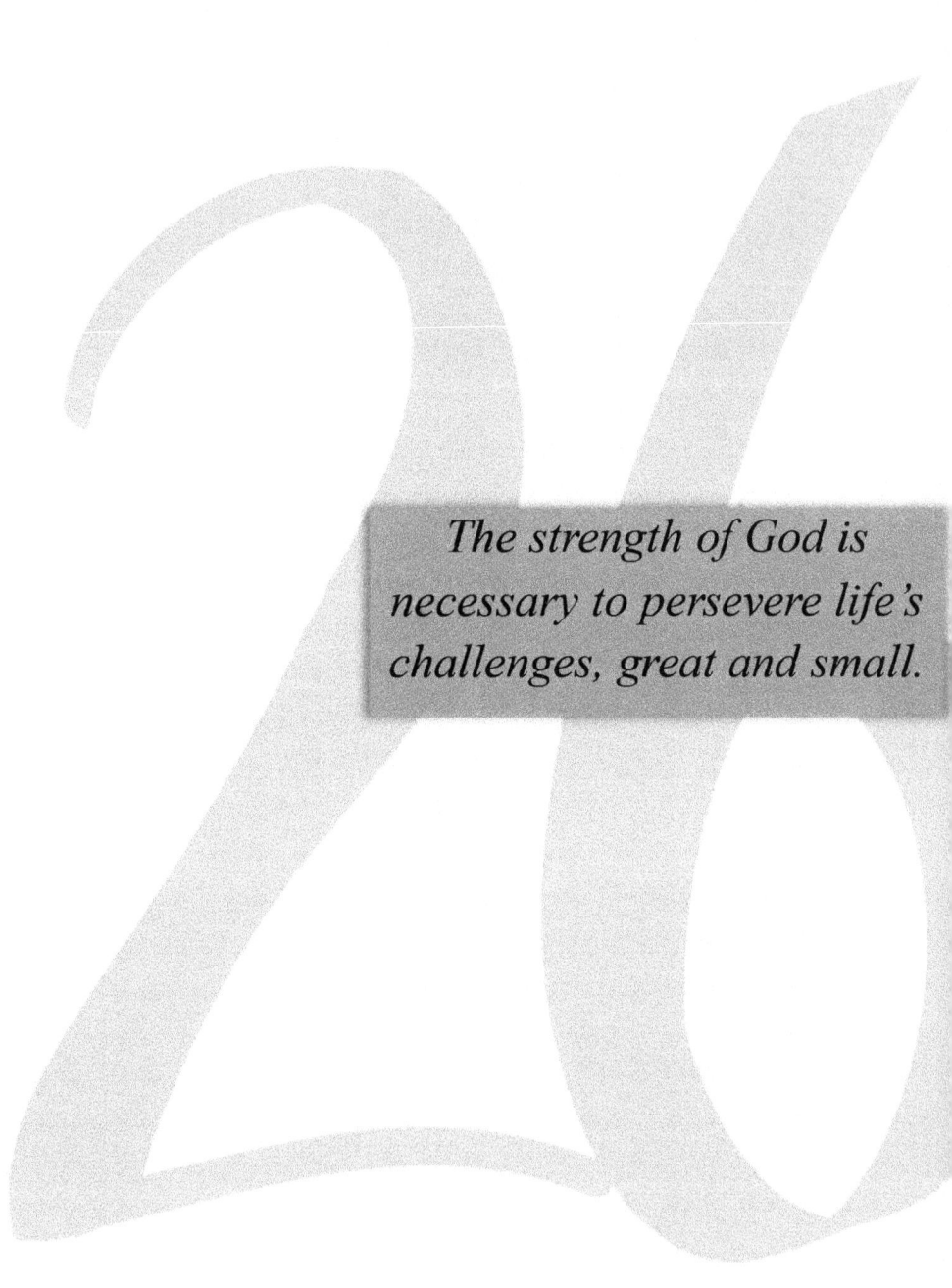

The strength of God is necessary to persevere life's challenges, great and small.

Strength

"The Lord is my light and my salvation; whom shall I fear? the Lord is the strength of my life; of whom shall I be afraid?"
Psalm 27:1 (KJV)

Father God, in the name of Jesus, Lord, I pray that your strength be perfect in my weakness. Lord, I pray that you will forever be the strength of my life and that the joy of the Lord will be my strength. Lord, I thank you for loving me enough never to forsake me. Lord, I pray that you will give me strength to handle any circumstance and overcome any situation in my life. Lord, your word tells me I can do all things through Christ who strengthens me. Lord, be my strength in the storm. Lord, be my strength when I'm happy and when I'm sad. Lord, I do not want to do life or attempt to live my journey without your strength, and empowerment. Lord be my refuge; Lord be my hiding place. Lord strengthen me and I will rejoice for your firm and mighty presence in my life.

I decree and declare I will rely on God's strength daily.

My Prayer Breakthrough Strategy

THE ENEMY....
_____
_____
_____
_____
_____
_____

MY BATTLEGROUND....
_____
_____
_____
_____
_____
_____

THE ENEMY'S STRATEGY....
_____
_____
_____
_____
_____
_____

MY PLAN OF ACTION....
_____
_____
_____
_____
_____

27

Choosing to forgive is a beautiful burden to live free from unforgiveness.

Overcoming Unforgiveness

"And be ye kind one to another, tenderhearted, forgiving one another, even as God for Christ's sake hath forgiven you."
Ephesians 4:32 (KJV)

Father, in the name of Jesus, you have forgiven me countless times, too many to recall. Lord, I ask you to help me to forgive others who have wronged me, betrayed me, offended me, lied to me, cheated me, abused me, hurt me in any way, mentally, physically, and emotionally. Lord, I fall out of agreement with all unforgiveness, rejection, anger, and bitterness. Lord, help me and free me from all traumatic experiences from my past and present. Lord, I pray that your love will help me not to walk in fear of being hurt by anyone. Lord, free me from any walls in my life constructed by unforgiveness. Lord, I thank you for helping me release everyone off the hook who has wronged me. Lord, I thank you that you have forgiven much so that I can forgive much in Jesus's name.

> **I decree and declare that God's love is being perfected in me to forgive all those who have offended me.**

My Prayer Breakthrough Strategy

THE ENEMY....
_____
_____
_____
_____
_____
_____

MY BATTLEGROUND....
_____
_____
_____
_____
_____
_____

THE ENEMY'S STRATEGY....
_____
_____
_____
_____
_____
_____

MY PLAN OF ACTION....
_____
_____
_____
_____
_____

A genuine love for God will always be evident in the love we show for one another.

Walking In Love

"...walk in love, as Christ also hath loved us, and hath given himself for us an offering and a sacrifice to God for a sweetsmelling savour."
Ephesians 5:2 (KJV)

Father, in the name of Jesus, I pray that you will help me to walk in love with everyone. Lord, I pray that your love will be reflected in my life daily. Lord, help me to love unconditionally. Lord, I pray for a revelation of love. Lord, help me to grow in love. As you have set the standard for love, I look to you Lord that loving my neighbor as myself would be a priority. Lord, I pray for grace and the capacity to love others as you have loved us. Lord, let my conversation be filled with love. Lord, I pray that you will cause my actions to be fueled by love. Lord, your word says, "...God is love."(I John 4:8) So, Lord, let your love be great in me so that I can love great. Lord, I thank you for your love.

I decree and declare the love of God is growing in my life daily.

My Prayer Breakthrough Strategy

THE ENEMY....
_____
_____
_____
_____
_____
_____

MY BATTLEGROUND....
_____
_____
_____
_____
_____
_____

THE ENEMY'S STRATEGY....
_____
_____
_____
_____
_____
_____

MY PLAN OF ACTION....
_____
_____
_____
_____
_____

29

Jesus took on shame so that you and I will not have to live with the painful harassment shame provides. Receive what Jesus did for you to live free from shame.

Shame

"Looking unto Jesus the author and finisher of our faith; who for the joy that was set before him endured the cross, despising the shame, and is set down at the right hand of the throne of God."
Hebrews 12:2 (KJV)

Father, I thank you for your everlasting love toward me. Lord, I thank you that I'm not what I've been through, nor am I defined by past mistakes. Lord, thank you for freeing me from self-hurt, self-pity, low self-esteem, condemnation, and shame. Father, your love is never-ending. I thank you for your unconditional love. I pray that your purpose will remain before me all the days of my life. Father, in the name of Jesus, I pray against every attack on my life's purpose and your plan for my life. I pray that I will be and do everything you purpose for me to do. I pray for boldness to be a light in a dark world. I thank you for being the lifter up of my head and removing shame from me in Jesus's name.

> **I declare I will not allow shame to ruin my life or rob me of my destiny.**

My Prayer Breakthrough Strategy

THE ENEMY....
_____
_____
_____
_____
_____

MY BATTLEGROUND....
_____
_____
_____
_____
_____

THE ENEMY'S STRATEGY....
_____
_____
_____
_____
_____

MY PLAN OF ACTION....
_____
_____
_____
_____
_____

Anger is the companion of fools. Don't allow it to contaminate your character, conduct, and conversation.

Anger and Rage

"Be not hasty in thy spirit to be angry: for anger resteth in the bosom of fools."
Ecclesiastes 7:9 (KJV)

Father, in the name of Jesus, I humble myself before you. I submit all of my ways to you. Your word says your ways are not like ours or our thoughts like yours. Lord, I pray that your ways be perfected in me and that I will take on the mind of Christ. Lord, I submit and surrender to you my attitude and behavior. Lord, I pray that I will exercise emotional intelligence. Father, give me the wisdom to recognize my triggers so that I may flee from any potential situations that can lead me to be angry. Lord, remove from me all strife, anger, rage, hurt, pride, bitterness, offense, and evil. Lord, I ask that you would create in me a clean heart and renew the right spirit in me that I may walk in your righteousness. Lord, your word says anger rest in the bosom of fools. As I strive to walk in wisdom daily Lord, help me be quick to forgive and let go of anything that leads to anger and rage. Lord, let your peace abide in me. Lord, I pray that your spirit will lead me in all truth. Lord, help me to resist the enemy that desires to destroy me. I pray that I will not allow anger to govern my conduct, character, or conversations in Jesus's name.

I decree and declare I will not allow anger to rule or dictate my attitude and actions.

My Prayer Breakthrough Strategy

THE ENEMY....
_____
_____
_____
_____
_____
_____

MY BATTLEGROUND....
_____
_____
_____
_____
_____
_____

THE ENEMY'S STRATEGY....
_____
_____
_____
_____
_____
_____

MY PLAN OF ACTION....
_____
_____
_____
_____
_____
_____

Biography of Jack Carter, Jr.

Jack Carter, Jr., a native of Chicago, Illinois, is an ordained minister of the gospel. He is widely recognized for his fervent passion for prayer. As the founder of the prayer room, Jack believes that his purpose and mission are to ignite a culture of prayer. Currently, he serves as the Prayer Leader of One Kingdom Ministries, located in San Antonio, Texas. His unwavering commitment to prayer and intercession has had a tremendous impact globally, touching and transforming countless lives. Jack and his wife, Natasha, have been happily married for 23 years and are the proud parents of three children: Faith, Knowledge, and Joy.

www.ingramcontent.com/pod-product-compliance
Lightning Source LLC
LaVergne TN
LVHW061555070526
838199LV00077B/7062